JO

MONSTERS
of Land

MW01074769

# red rhino books®

## NONFICTION

## SADDLEBACK
### EDUCATIONAL PUBLISHING
www.sdlback.com

All source images from Shutterstock.com

ISBN-13: 978-1-68021-030-9
ISBN-10: 1-68021-030-0
eBook: 978-1-63078-337-2

Printed in Malaysia

20 19 18 17 16    2 3 4 5 6

# TABLE OF CONTENTS

# Chapter 1
# WHAT'S THAT?

*Woof! Woof! Woof!*
Dogs bark.
Their howls fill the air.
A woman looks out the window.

It's dark.
Too dark to see.
Something *shrieks*.
Dogs growl.
Their cries *scare* the woman.
Something is out there.
But what?

The woman walks outside.
She sees something.
It is in the woods!
What is it?
A shadow?

It looks like an animal.
Could it be a bobcat?
No. It's too big.
The woman goes inside.
She hides in bed.
She is scared.
She can't sleep.

The dogs cry.
Then they stop.
All is silent.

5

*Rap! Rap! Rap!*
It is morning.
Someone is at the woman's door.
She opens it.
Police officers stand there.

They want to know about last night.
They ask if she heard anything.
She tells them about the dogs.
She says she saw a large cat.

They shake their heads.

They tell her the news.

Four dogs are dead.

The dogs were killed.

Their jaws were broken.

Their blood was *drained*.

The woman gasps.

"Was it the Beast of Bladenboro?" she asks.

"Did it strike again?"

"There's no such thing," a cop says.

The woman knows better.

DO NOT CROS

Everyone in Bladenboro,
North Carolina, knows better.
They all know about the monster.
They fear it.

AN EVIL BEAST

People say it's a *vampire*.
It drinks animals' blood.
It rips their skin.
It crushes their heads.

The woman is sure.
The beast killed those dogs.

Did it?
Is the Beast of Bladenboro real?
Maybe.
Maybe not.
You decide.

# Chapter 2
# MONSTER HUNTERS

Every place seems to have a monster.

The Jersey Devil.

The Wolfman of Chestnut Mountain.

Bigfoot! Yeti! Mothman!

Have you heard the stories?

Monsters come in all shapes.

Some look like apes.

Some have big *fangs*.

Some fly.

Others *slither*.

People see monsters.

They tell stories.

But no one has ever caught one.

Not ever.

You can watch movies about monsters.

You can read about them in books.

But are any monsters real?

People want to know.

Some even chase monsters.

They try to find them.

They are monster hunters.

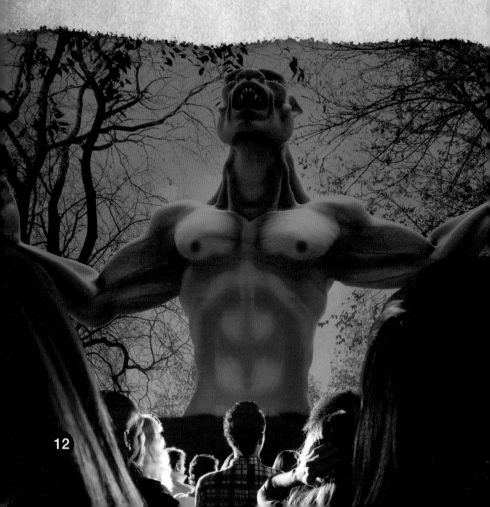

Monster hunters look in forests.

They look in the jungle.

They look in *swamps*.

Loren Coleman is a monster hunter.

He looks for Bigfoot.

Bigfoot is a big, hairy monster.

People say it lives in forests.

John "Tapper" Tice hunts monsters
in West Virginia.
He looks for them in the mountains.
He films a TV show about them.
He wants to *prove* monsters exist.
He would feel lucky to catch one.
Would you?
Do you want to catch a monster?

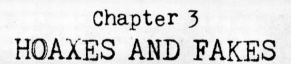

# Chapter 3
# HOAXES AND FAKES

Some monsters are *myths*.

Ancient Greeks told many stories.

Some were about monsters.

One was the griffin.

It had a lion's body.

It had an eagle's head.

Some monsters are *hoaxes*.
The stories are made up.
Ever heard of the Cardiff Giant?
It was a famous monster hoax.

The lie started in 1869.
Workers dug up something in
Cardiff, New York.
George Hull said it was the body
of a giant.
It looked very old.

People paid to see the giant.
But they soon learned it was a fake.
The giant was carved out of rock.
Hull paid a man to do it.
He wanted to fool people.

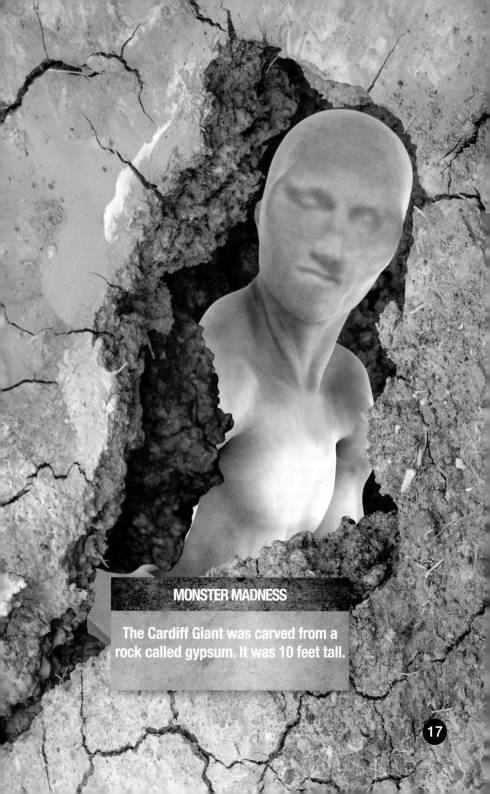

## MONSTER MADNESS

The Cardiff Giant was carved from a rock called gypsum. It was 10 feet tall.

There was another famous hoax.
It was 1959.
People said they saw a monster.
Its eyes glowed.
It stood 9 feet tall.

The monster lurked near
Brooksville, Florida.
It came. It went.
But no one could find it.
It was a *mystery*.

Two newspaper reporters looked.
They asked questions.
Then they found the monster.
But it wasn't real.

Peggy Thomas had made it.
She used a cow skull for its head.
She used a flashlight for its eyes.
It was a joke, Peggy said.
Just a joke.

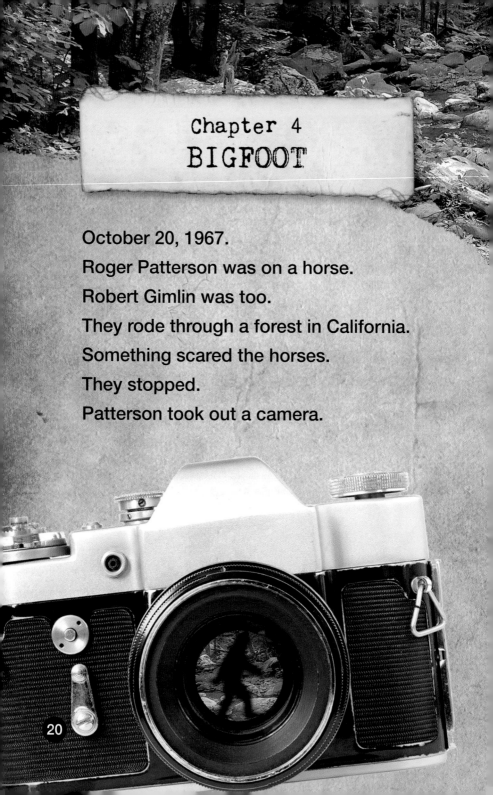

## Chapter 4
# BIGFOOT

October 20, 1967.

Roger Patterson was on a horse.

Robert Gimlin was too.

They rode through a forest in California.

Something scared the horses.

They stopped.

Patterson took out a camera.

He pointed it toward a creek.

Something was there.

It was a creature.

It was big and hairy.

It looked like an ape.

It walked on two legs.

People saw the film.

Some didn't believe it was real.

Others said it was "Bigfoot."

What is Bigfoot?

It is an ape-like creature.

It lives in the forest.

It has large eyes and a round head.

It leaves big footprints.

There are many stories about this monster.

Some go back a long time.

Native Americans believe in Bigfoot.

They call it Sasquatch.

BIGFOOT; SASQUATCH

Mystery, Myth, or Real:
**Mystery**

Location:
**Pacific Northwest; Other States**

Evidence:
**Footprints; Eyewitness Stories**

Is Bigfoot real?
Who knows?
There's no proof.

Some have lied.
One man made fake footprints.
Another said he shot Bigfoot.
No one ever saw a body.
It was a hoax.

But monster hunters still search.
And people still tell stories.

# Chapter 5
# YETI

Nepal is in Asia.

People there tell stories of a creature.

They call it the Wild Man of the Snows.

You may know it as

the Abominable Snowman.

Most people call it the Yeti.

The Yeti looks like an ape.

It walks on two legs.

It has long, dark hair.

It leaves footprints in the snow.

**MONSTER MADNESS**

Alexander the Great heard stories
of the Yeti 2,300 years ago.

CLOSE-UP

25

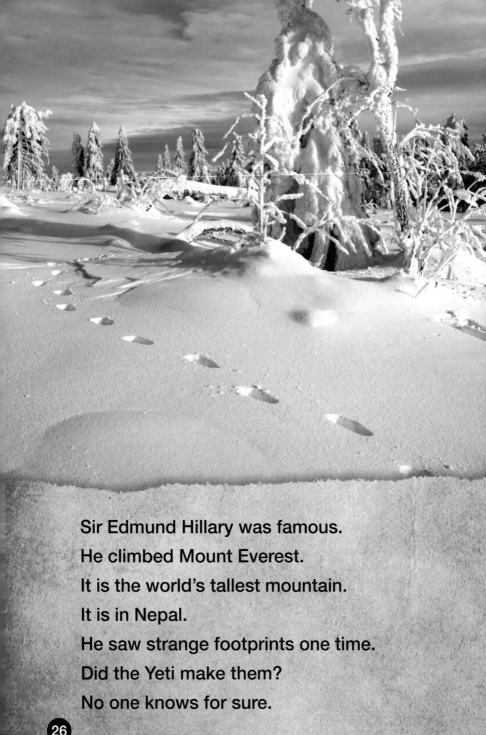

Sir Edmund Hillary was famous.

He climbed Mount Everest.

It is the world's tallest mountain.

It is in Nepal.

He saw strange footprints one time.

Did the Yeti make them?

No one knows for sure.

## YETI; ABOMINABLE SNOWMAN; WILD MAN OF THE SNOWS

**Mystery, Myth, or Real:**
**Mystery**

**Location:**
**Nepal; Tibet; Other Regions**

**Evidence:**
**Footprints; Eyewitness Stories; Hair and Bones**

Hillary later looked for the beast.

He could not find it.

Someone found part of an animal's head.

Hillary wanted to know if it was the Yeti's.

Was it?

No.

It was an antelope *scalp.*

Some say the Yeti is a myth.
A story parents tell their children.

Some say the Yeti is real.
But you have to believe.
That is the only way to see it.

Do you believe?

## Chapter 6
# BEAST OF BRAY ROAD

Wisconsin has a lot of farms.

It has country roads.

One is Bray Road.

People have seen a monster there.

They call it the Beast of Bray Road.

Three girls said they saw the beast.

It had pointy ears.

It had large claws.

Its fur was dark.

They said it looked like a *werewolf*.

Half man. Half wolf.

A reporter heard the tale.

She talked to people.

Each said the same thing.

*The Bray Road Beast lives!*

Other people said they saw the creature.

Some said it ran fast.

They said it left strange footprints.

Stories about the beast spread.

But no one could find it.

It came and went.

Was it a coyote?

Was it a wolf?

No, people said.

Those animals don't run on two feet.

## MONSTER MADNESS

Reports of the Beast of Bray Road made it famous. A movie came out in 2005 with the same name.

Native Americans have a name for the beast.

*Shunka warak' in*.

It means "carrying off dogs."

The girls saw the beast in the 1990s.

Time has passed.

No one has seen it in years.

Was it ever really there?

You decide.

BEAST OF BRAY ROAD;
SHUNKA WARAK' IN

Mystery, Myth, or Real: **Mystery**

Location: **Wisconsin**

Evidence: **Footprints; Eyewitness Stories**

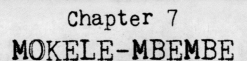

# Chapter 7
# MOKELE-MBEMBE

Are dinosaurs still alive?

They can't be.

They died long ago.

But people in Africa are not so sure.

They talk about a dinosaur.

They call it *Mokele-mbembe*.

What does its name mean?

"One who stops the flow of rivers."

**MONSTER MADNESS**

Dinosaurs died out
65 million years ago.

The monster is 35 feet long.

Its skin is brown.

It has a long neck.

It lives in caves along rivers.

It eats elephants.

It eats hippos.

People once saw Mokele-mbembe
from an airplane.
It was swimming in a lake.
They shot a movie.
The picture was fuzzy.
Was it an elephant?
Was it a hippo?
Was it a person in a *canoe*?
No one knows.

Could some dinosaurs still be around?
People want to know.
They look for bones.
They look for teeth.
They look for tracks.

They look for Mokele-mbembe.
But no one has found it yet.

MOKELE-MBEMBE

Mystery, Myth, or Real:
**Mystery**

Location: **Africa**

Evidence:
**Eyewitness Stories**

# Chapter 8
# MOTHMAN

What about flying monsters?

People in West Virginia talk about one.

One boy said he saw an angel.

One woman said she saw a giant butterfly.

It shrieked. It ate dogs.

It scared people.

People began calling it "Mothman."

People kept seeing Mothman.

It stayed for a year.

Then something bad happened.

## MONSTER MADNESS

Point Pleasant, West Virginia,
has a Mothman Museum.

MOTHMAN

Mystery, Myth, or Real: **Mystery**

Location: **West Virginia**

Evidence:
**Eyewitness Stories**

It was December 15, 1967.

A bridge fell into the Ohio River.

Dozens died.

Some blamed Mothman.

Others said the beast came to *warn* people.

Some said Mothman was a *curse*.

It was sent by Chief Cornstalk.

He was a Native American.

He was killed in 1777.

Some think he wanted to get even.

They say he sent Mothman.

Mothman left after the bridge fell.
It was never seen again.
But people still talk about it.
They put up a *statue*.
It is in the center of town.

# Chapter 9
# FLORIDA SKUNK APE

Dave Shealy saw a monster.

It was 1974.

He was 10.

He and his brother were outside.

They lived by a Florida swamp.

His brother saw it first.

It was a strange creature.

It was covered in hair.

Dave saw it next.

They called it a skunk ape.

Dave saw the creature again.

One. Two. Three times.

He filmed one on *video*.

The skunk ape stood about 6 feet tall.
It was furry.
It looked like Bigfoot.

Why is it called a skunk ape?

It smells bad.

Like a skunk.

Like rotten eggs.

Scientists say the creature is not real.

They say it is a myth.

No one has ever found one.

But Dave believes.

He's seen the monster.

He wants to see it again.

## FLORIDA SKUNK APE

Mystery, Myth, or Real:
**Mystery or Myth**

Location: **Florida**

Evidence:
**Eyewitness Stories**

### MONSTER MADNESS

Some people think there is more than one skunk ape. Seven to nine might live in Florida's Everglades.

# Chapter 10
# LIZARD MAN

South Carolina has a swamp monster too.

It stands 7 feet high.

Its eyes glow red.

It looks like a *lizard*.

A lizard man.

It has three fingers on each hand.

It rips apart cars with its claws.

The monster has been seen in Lee County.

It was first spotted in 1986.

People found traces of its blood.

They found footprints with three toes.

Police looked into the reports.

They said it was a bear.

But no one knows for sure.

# LIZARD MAN

Mystery, Myth, or Real:
**Mystery**

Location: **South Carolina**

Evidence: **Eyewitness Stories; Damaged Cars**

Do you believe in monsters?
Many do.

    **The Beast of Bladenboro**
    **Bigfoot**
    **Yeti**
    **The Beast of Bray Road**
    **Mokele-mbembe**
    **Mothman**
    **Florida Skunk Ape**
    **Lizard Man**

All are monsters.
People say they have seen them.
Some hunt them.
Will they find them?
Time will tell.

# GLOSSARY

**canoe:** long, narrow boat

**curse:** ask a magical power to harm someone

**drained:** caused the liquid to run out

**fangs:** long, pointed teeth

**gypsum:** a soft white mineral

**hoaxes:** stories that are fake

**lizard:** a cold-blooded animal with a tail

**mystery:** a puzzling event

**myths:** ancient stories that are not true

**prove:** to establish the truth of something

scalp: skin on top of a head

scare: to make someone afraid

shriek: cry out loudly

slither: to slide along

statue: a model of an animal, person, or thing made out of stone or metal

swamps: land that is always wet with lots of plants

vampire: a monster that drinks blood

video: moving pictures that have been recorded

warn: tell somebody of a dangerous situation

werewolf: a human who turns into a wolf

# TAKE A LOOK INSIDE

# MONSTERS OF THE DEEP

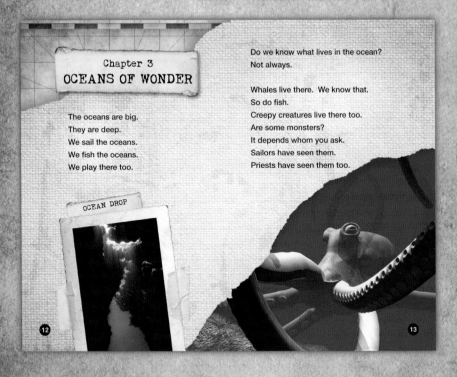

### Chapter 3
## OCEANS OF WONDER

The oceans are big.
They are deep.
We sail the oceans.
We fish the oceans.
We play there too.

OCEAN DROP

Do we know what lives in the ocean?
Not always.

Whales live there.  We know that.
So do fish.
Creepy creatures live there too.
Are some monsters?
It depends whom you ask.
Sailors have seen them.
Priests have seen them too.

Giant squid have strong teeth and a beak.
Their jaws break food into tiny bites.
They hunt for fish. Not sailors.
They crush sharks. Not ships.

Giant squid are *mollusks*.
They don't have a *spine*.
They are rare.
Fishermen found one in 2007.
It was 992 pounds.

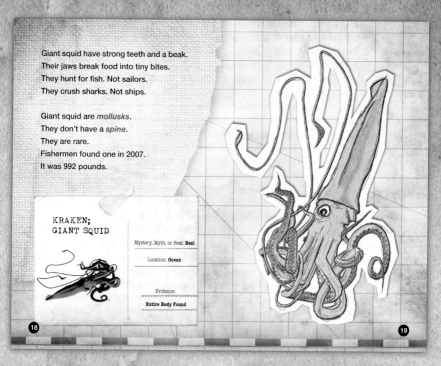

KRAKEN;
GIANT SQUID

Mystery, Myth, or Real: **Real**

Location: **Ocean**

Evidence:
**Entire Body Found**

**MONSTER MADNESS**

The serpent wiggled like a caterpillar
as it swam.

SEA SERPENT
OF GLOUCESTER

Mystery, Myth, or Real:
**Mystery**

Location: **Gloucester, MA**

Evidence:
**Eyewitness Stories**

They said it was a sea serpent.
A man shot at it from a boat.
He missed.
The monster went away.
It returned many times.
People swear they saw a serpent.
It has never been seen again.

# red rhino books®

## NONFICTION

9781680210293

9781680210286

9781680210309

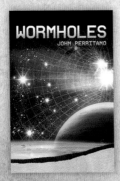

9781680210330

9781680210361

9781680210323

9781680210316

9781680210538

9781680210347

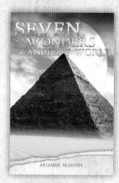

9781680210354

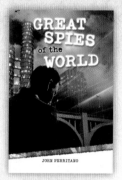

9781680210491

9781680210521

9781680210378

9781680210484

MORE
TITLES
COMING
SOON